This Coloring Book Belongs To

_____

Thank you so much for choosing our book. We hope you enjoy it to the fullest!

Dive into the wonderful world of cows with our **Cow Coloring Book for Adults**! These captivating creatures have been an integral part of human history and development for thousands of years. Originating from the Indian subcontinent and scientifically known as Bos taurus, cows have not only provided us with valuable products like milk, meat, and leather but have also been companions in agriculture and rural life. With their calm presence and serene gaze, they remind us of the beauty and tranquility of nature.

In this coloring book, we celebrate the majesty of cows with 50 detailed illustrations that capture their essence in natural settings. From rolling pastures to bucolic landscapes, these pages invite you to explore the serenity and calmness these creatures exude.

Get ready to embark on a journey of color and discovery as you breathe life into these charming cows with your own unique touch of color! Dive into this **Cow Coloring Book for Adults** and let yourself be carried away by the serenity and beauty of these wonderful creatures.

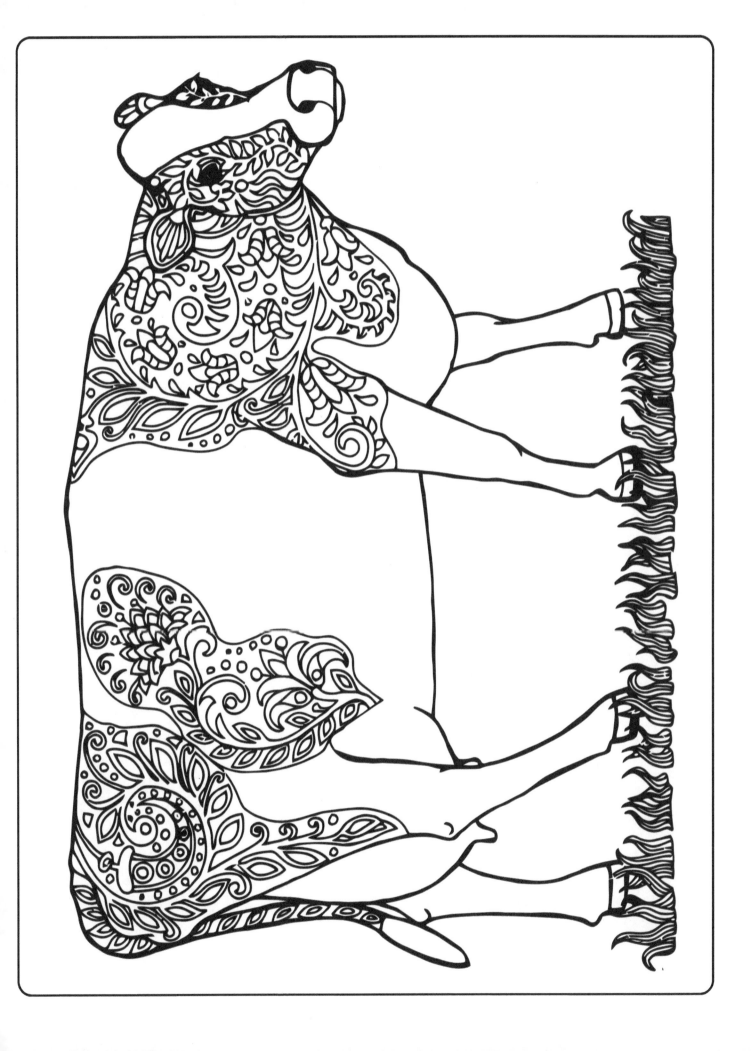

Dear reader,

We're delighted to know you've chosen our coloring book to accompany you on your creative journey. Your time and dedication are truly appreciated.

As a newly established publisher, every review we receive is a guiding light on our path toward growth and continuous improvement.

If you have a moment, we would love to hear your thoughts about our book on Amazon. Your opinion is invaluable and will help other readers discover the joy and inspiration this book can offer.

We're eager to hear your thoughts and look forward to reading your review. Thank you for being part of our creative community!

With gratitude,

Kary Hawthorne

SCAN ME!

Made in United States
Troutdale, OR
10/28/2024

24222441R00058